Imran Learns

About Ramadan

Sajda Nazlee

Ta-Ha Publishers Ltd.
1 Wynne Road
London
SW9 0BB

Published by:
Ta-Ha Publishers Ltd.
1 Wynne Road
London SW9 0BB

Website: http://www.taha.co.uk
Email: sales@taha.co.uk

Written by: Sajda Nazlee
Edited by: Dr. Abia Afsar-Siddiqui
Illustrated by: M. Ishaq

A catalogue record of this book is available from the British Library.

ISBN: 1 842000 70 5

Printed and bound by: De-Luxe Printers Ltd., London

Imran Learns About Ramadan

It was four o'clock in the morning! Imran was fast asleep under his duvet when suddenly he woke up with a start. There were noises coming from the kitchen just underneath his bedroom. He opened his eyes and saw that the light was on in the hallway.

"Who can that be in the kitchen at this time of night?" he asked himself. "Why is the hallway light on? Surely mother and father are asleep. They always turn out all the lights before they go to sleep."

He found it difficult to imagine that burglars would be so stupid as to turn on all the lights and make a lot of noise. But he couldn't think of anyone else who would be up at this time of night.

Slowly he crept out of bed and made his way cautiously down the stairs. He told himself, "If there really are burglars I will frighten them off with the karate I have learnt. Then everyone will congratulate me for being so brave." Now he rather hoped that there really were burglars in the house although he knew enough to be scared as well.

He tiptoed down to the bottom of the stairs. There he found that the kitchen light was on as well. Imran could hear voices in the kitchen.

"How many of them are there?" he thought to himself preparing for action.

He pushed the kitchen door open gently ready to surprise the thieves.

But instead, Imran himself got the surprise! He found his mother and father in the kitchen eating a meal! At four o'clock in the morning!

"As salaamu alaikum, Imran," said his mother and father. Then all three of them said at the same time, "What are you doing up so early?" and they all laughed.

"Wa alaikum salaam, father and mother," Imran said walking towards the table, "I thought that you were burglars. I was about to do my karate moves on you!"

"Oh, Imran!" his mother laughed, "Didn't I tell you that the month of Ramadan is starting? All the Muslims all over the world have started fasting today. Everyone is waking up before dawn to eat a little before the day begins."

"Yes, of course! Now I remember," Imran said in surprise, because he had completely forgotten. He sat down at the table.

Imran's mother had told him that Ramadan is the ninth month of the Islamic calendar. Muslims know that a new month has started when they see the thin new moon in the sky just after the setting of the sun. The day after that is the first day of the new month.

Imran's mother explained that throughout the month of Ramadan, Muslims should not eat or drink during the day; that means from Fajr time before dawn until Maghrib time just after sunset. The Arabic word for fasting is *sawm*. To help Muslims fast, Allah has asked us to eat a meal before Fajr time, which is called *suhoor*. So Imran's parents were eating their *suhoor* meal.

"Father," Imran began, "Why do Muslims fast?"

"We fast because Allah ordered us to fast in the Qur'an," his father said.

"That was a very simple answer," Imran thought.

"Ramadan is a very special month full of *barakah* for Muslims all over the world," his father continued.

"What is *barakah*?" Imran asked. Like children everywhere he was always full of questions. His father didn't mind his questions too much. When he answered them they often had very interesting talks and Imran learned a lot.

"*Barakah* is the Arabic word for blessing, Imran," he said, "This is something nice and good which is a special gift from Allah. He gives this gift to someone or something that He loves. Allah puts a lot of blessings and good into Ramadan. Allah is merciful and kind, but in Ramadan He is especially kind and this is a time when, if we are good, then we can have *barakah* too."

"Also fasting is good for us in lots of ways," his mother said. "If we didn't fast we might forget how it feels not to have anything to eat or drink like very poor people."

When we know what it feels like not be able to eat and drink for a few hours, it makes us want to thank Allah for all that He has given us instead of complaining that we do not have enough. We learn not to be greedy and selfish."

"We learn all that?" asked Imran.

"Actually," said his father, "We learn even more than that. When we fast, as well as not eating and drinking, we also have to be extra careful not to tell lies or say mean things about people behind their back. We should be extra kind and generous to everyone. That is good training for the rest of the year."

"I want to fast, too. Can I fast today, father, please?" Imran begged, eager to join in with the adults. "Please, just for half a day?"

"Not today, Imran," his mother answered quickly, "Because the time for the meal of *suhoor* is almost over. I don't want you to fast without eating something first. Anyway, I didn't wake you up because it is a school day today."

Imran must have looked very disappointed because she quickly added, "Insha'Allah you can fast tomorrow when it is the weekend", and he cheered up.

True to her word, the next day his mother woke
Imran up at the time of *suhoor* to have
the early breakfast.

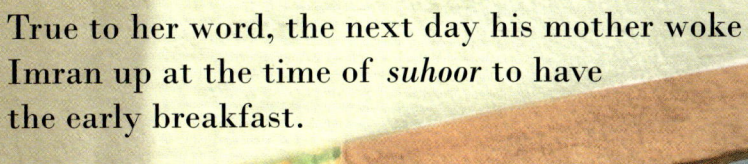

When he had finished eating and drinking he said, "I
intend to fast this fast of Ramadan." His
mother had told him how important it was to
remember to make the intention to fast.
Then he made his wudu, said his Fajr
prayer and went to sleep.

Later in the morning, at around ten o'clock when Imran had woken up, he went to see Mrs. Ali, because she was not very well. Mrs. Ali was his headmaster's mother. She liked an excuse to have Imran around and Imran also liked Mrs. Ali's company. Sometimes Imran's mother helped Mrs. Ali with the housework and the shopping. Imran always liked helping Mrs. Ali. His mother had told him that Allah is very pleased with Muslims who help other people for the sake of Allah.

When Imran reached Mrs. Ali's house he was very surprised and shocked to find her eating.

"As salaamu alaikum, Mrs. Ali," he said, but he was too embarrassed to say to an elder like Mrs. Ali, "Why are you eating? Why are you not fasting?"

She seemed to read his mind because she said, "Wa alaikum salaam, Imran. I am sure you are wondering why I am not fasting today. It's because I am ill. The doctor has given me some medicines which I have to take during the day, so I cannot fast."

"Oh!" said Imran in surprise, "I thought that Allah wants all adults to fast."

"Yes, Allah orders all adults to fast. But Allah allows people who are poorly not to fast. They can make up their fasts another time," Mrs. Ali replied. "And Allah allows people who are travelling to do the same."

Imran must still have looked confused for she continued, "Allah is merciful. He wants us to look after ourselves. If we make ourselves more ill then Allah is very angry with us. I am unwell at the moment and cannot fast during this month. So I will fast afterwards when I am better, to make up for what I have missed."

"Oh I see," said Imran, "I didn't know that. Mrs. Ali, you must look after yourself well. You must not make Allah angry with you."

"Thank you, Imran. I will look after myself," she said, smiling to him.

Imran returned home and played for a while on the swing in the back garden. After a short time he began to feel hungry and thirsty. Of course it had completely slipped his mind why he was hungry. He had not eaten since before the first light of dawn. He had forgotten that he was fasting. So he made his way towards the fruit bowl in the living room.

Imran never ate alone. He had learnt not to just go and take food for himself. Muslims, he knew, sat and ate together with other people. But today was very unusual. Today, he was very hungry. So he took some grapes from the fruit bowl.

As he was finishing the last grape he suddenly remembered just why he was so hungry. "I'm fasting!" he thought, "*Astaghfirullah* (I ask Allah to forgive me)! I was supposed to be fasting!" Iman panicked.

Just then he heard his mother somewhere in the house and he rushed off to find her. "Mother, mother!" he cried, really upset, "Where are you?"

"What on earth has happened, Imran?" asked his mother, "Why are you crying?"

"Oh mother, Allah is going to be angry with me. I forgot that I was fasting and ate some grapes," said Imran, rubbing his tearful eyes.

"Calm down, Imran," she said, "Allah is not angry at you, because you ate accidentally. I think that He will definitely forgive you. He becomes angry when we do something wrong and we know that it is wrong."

Imran calmed down.

"It was Allah who fed you when you forgot that you were fasting," she said, "The important thing to remember is that you stopped as soon as you remembered you were fasting."

Imran felt a little better. He had only forgotten by accident. Allah was not angry. It was Allah who had fed him. He was amazed at this.

Imran thought about people trying a little harder in this month to please Allah. His mother had told him that the Prophet ﷺ was very generous and giving in Ramadan. Imran decided that it would be a good time to save money and give it to those poor people who find it difficult to buy enough food to eat.

His thoughts were interrupted by his mother calling out to him, "It's one o'clock now. You have fasted for half a day. Now let me make you something to eat."

Imran felt very pleased with himself at having fasted for half a day and he couldn't wait to tell his father.

"Before you eat," reminded his mother, "Don't forget to thank Allah for all His blessings."

So Imran thanked Allah and said 'Bismillah' before munching away on his sandwiches.

When Imran went to school on Monday, he found out that a lot of his friends at school were also fasting for a half day. They normally had some money with them to have milk and biscuits in their break time.

Imran thought that it would be a good idea to ask his friends to save that money on the days they were fasting so that they could give it to the poor.

Imran told his headmaster, Mr. Ali, about his idea and Mr. Ali was very pleased. That morning he made an announcement in morning assembly about it. He told the children that if they wanted to take part, they should ask their parents' permission and then give the money to their class teacher for safe keeping.

By the end of the week, all the class teachers had collected quite a lot of money and Mr. Ali gave it all to charity on Imran's behalf.

That night, Imran went home with a very special feeling inside and he couldn't stop smiling. He asked his father why he was feeling like this.

"Every time you do something nice for other people, then Allah is very pleased with you," said his father. "When Allah is pleased with you, then that is the best feeling in the world."

"What else can I do to please Allah?" asked Imran eagerly. He wanted to carry on having this special feeling inside him.

"There are so many things that you can do to please Allah. But the important thing to remember is that whatever you do should only be for the pleasure of Allah, not to show off in front of other people," explained Imran's father.

"So what can I do?" asked Imran impatiently.

"You can read the Qur'an even more during Ramadan. Did you know that Ramadan is also called the month of the Qur'an?" said Imran's father.

"What does that mean?" asked Imran. He was confused because he thought that Ramadan was the month of fasting.

"Allah tells us in the Qur'an itself that Ramadan was the month in which Allah sent the Qur'an down to the Prophet Muhammad ﷺ," said Imran's father pointing out the verse in the Qur'an.

"So you will get extra reward from Allah for reciting and studying the Qur'an in Ramadan, especially while you are fasting," continued Imran's father.

So, Imran made sure that he sat down with his mother to recite a bit of the Qur'an every single day during Ramadan.

On some evenings, Imran's parents invited other people to their house for *iftar*, to break the fast with them. It was so nice to break the fast and share the special feeling of Ramadan with other people. Imran always helped his parents to prepare the evening meal because he knew that would please Allah.

One afternoon, Imran saw his parents preparing for *iftar*. "Why do we always break the fast with dates?" asked Imran.

"The Prophet ﷺ always broke his fast by eating dates or by drinking water. So we try to do this too," explained Imran's mother. "It is tempting to eat too much after you have been fasting for a whole day but that is not good for you. Dates are a good way to break the fast."

"We also make *du'a* or pray to Allah when we break the fast as this is one of the best times to make *du'a* to Allah," said Imran's father.

That evening, just before Maghrib time, Imran sat down and made *du'a* to Allah. He thanked Allah for giving him so much. He asked Allah to look after his parents and family. He prayed for the people in the world that were not so lucky as him. When the time came to break the fast, Imran said '*Bismillah*', and ate some dates. Then Imran and his father performed their Maghrib prayer.

After they had eaten their evening meal, Imran's father was getting ready to go to the mosque.

"Can I come as well?" asked Imran. "We can do our Isha prayer together at the mosque."

"During Ramadan, there is a special prayer called *Tarawih*, which we do after Isha. This is quite long. Are you sure you want to come with me to the mosque?" asked Imran's father.

"I'd love to," said Imran and ran upstairs to do his wudu.

There were lots of people at the mosque, even some boys the same age as Imran. The prayers were long and the Imam recited a lot of the Qur'an. But Imran was thrilled to hear the beautiful recitation. Afterwards the Imam gave a small talk about the blessings of Ramadan.

There was so much to do in Ramadan and the days passed so quickly. Soon the month of Ramadan was over and it was Eid day.

On the morning of Eid, Imran ran down the stairs and shouted "Eid Mubarak!" to his parents. "Eid Mubarak to you too, Imran!"they replied. They all sat down to a light breakfast of dates and milk after sunrise.

"Go and have a shower and then put on your new clothes," said Imran's mother. "But don't be too long in the bathroom!"

When they were all ready, Imran and his parents walked to the mosque for the Eid prayer. There were enormous numbers of people there. Imran had never seen so many Muslims; men, women and children together. After the prayer, the Imam gave two talks or *khutbah*s in Arabic and English.

Then everybody turned and greeted everybody else with "As salaamu alaikum! Eid Mubarak!" Imran had never shaken so many hands or hugged so many people in all his life before.

Although it was a wonderful day of celebration, Imran was a little sad. "Why am I sad, mother?" he asked.

She smiled and said, "We are all a little sad, Imran, because Ramadan has gone for another year and we no longer have the blessings of Ramadan." And Imran knew that he would look forward to Ramadan coming again.

Ramadan Mubarak! The month of fasting
is here,
The month that we have been waiting for all year,
We must not eat or drink during the day,
And be especially careful about the things we say.
Fasting helps us to think of the poor and needy
And giving in charity stops us from
becoming greedy.
We should spend our time in the worship of Allah
So that we, too, can get the gift of barakah.

QUICK QUIZ

1. What is the Arabic word for fasting?

2. What is *barakah*?

3. What are some of the things that we learn from fasting?

4. Do you know why Ramadan is also called the Month of the Qur'an?

5. Why was Imran sad when Ramadan was over?